# EASTER
## is Special

Anita Gane...
& Jennie Po...

Published in 2014 by Wayland

Copyright © Wayland 2014

Wayland
338 Euston Road
London NW1 3BH

Wayland Australia
Level 17/207 Kent Street
Sydney, NSW 2000

Produced for Wayland by Calcium
Design: Emma DeBanks
Editor for Wayland: Victoria Brooker
Illustrations by Jennie Poh

British Library Cataloguing in Publication Data

Ganeri, Anita, 1961–
  Easter is special. — (Special)
  1. Easter—Juvenile literature.
  I. Title II. Series
  263.9'3-dc23

ISBN-13: 9780750284141

First published in 2013 by Wayland

Printed in China

Wayland is a division of Hachette Children's Books,
an Hachette UK company.

www.hachette.co.uk

# Contents

# It's Easter

Easter is a time of new life.
There are butterflies and flowers
everywhere. Best of all, there's an
Easter egg hunt to look forward to!

Cheep!

Cheep!

# Easter is Special

Easter is so special. It's the time when Jesus died and came back to life again.

Easter happens in springtime when new life is all around.

# A Better World

Christians believe that God sent Jesus to teach people about God. They believe that Jesus died to make the world a better place for us all.

The story of Easter is told in a special book, called the Bible.

# Before Easter

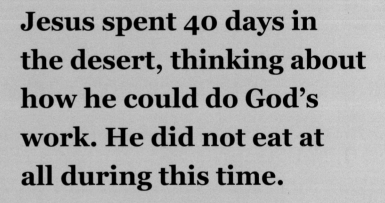

Jesus spent 40 days in the desert, thinking about how he could do God's work. He did not eat at all during this time.

The 40 days before Easter are called Lent. At Lent, we give up something we like to eat to remember how Jesus gave up food when he was in the desert.

11

# Pancake Day

At Lent, people used to eat plain food. They made pancakes before Lent to use up rich food, such as butter and eggs. We make pancakes on the first day before Lent begins. We call this day Shrove Tuesday. Sometimes, we have a pancake race, too!

# Ash Wednesday

The first day of Lent is Ash Wednesday. We go to a special service in church. The priest uses ash to draw a cross on our foreheads.

The ash cross is a way of saying sorry to God for the things we have done wrong.

# Holy Week

The week before Easter is called Holy Week. At this time, we remember the last week of Jesus's life on Earth. Holy Week begins on Palm Sunday.

On Palm Sunday, Jesus rode
into Jerusalem on a donkey.
People waved palm leaves
as he went past.

# Last Supper

On the Thursday of Holy Week, Jesus and his friends had their last meal together. Jesus gave them some bread to eat and some wine to drink. He told them not to forget about him.

# Jesus Dies

Jesus said that he was the Son of God. This made the rulers of Jerusalem angry. They nailed Jesus to a cross and left him to die. People feel sad remembering how Jesus died.

Jesus died on Good Friday. Good Friday means 'God's Friday'.

# Remember the Cross

At Easter, we eat hot cross buns. They have currants inside and a cross on top. The cross reminds us of how Jesus died.

Long ago, people baked hot-cross buns and gave them to poor people.

23

# Jesus Lives Again

Jesus's friends laid his body in a tomb. Two days later, they visited the tomb – and found it empty! An angel told them that Jesus had come back to life.

Later, Jesus appeared before his friends. They were frightened at first, but Jesus told them not to be scared.

Hope and joy

# Easter Eggs

At Easter, we hunt for chocolate eggs. The eggs remind us of Jesus's new life, and of all the other new lives we see in the spring.

27

Happy Easter

28

Easter Sunday is a happy day! It's the day on which Jesus came back to life. We go to church to say thank you to God for sending Jesus to Earth. Then we eat a special Easter meal.

# Another Special Day

Forty days after Easter, we remember another special time. It is called Ascension Day. This is when Jesus went up into Heaven to be with God forever.

In Heaven

# Glossary

**Christians** people who follow Jesus's teachings

**desert** a dry place with very little water

**Jesus** a holy teacher who lived thousands of years ago. Christians believe that he is the son of God.

**priest** a man who teaches people about God

**rulers** people who are in charge

**tomb** a place in which a body is buried

# Index